# SNORKEL CORAL REEFS

BY K.C. KELLEY

AMICUS READERS ● AMICUS INK

amicus
readers

Amicus Readers and Amicus Ink are imprints of Amicus
P.O. Box 1329, Mankato, MN 56002
www.amicuspublishing.us

Names: Kelley, K. C., author.
Title: Snorkel coral reefs / by K.C. Kelley.
Description: Mankato, MN : Amicus, [2018] l Series: Amazing animals
Identifiers: LCCN 2017022597 (print) l LCCN 2017031603 (ebook) l ISBN
  9781681513461 (pdf) l ISBN 9781681513102 (library binding : alk. paper) l
  ISBN 9781681522661 (pbk. : alk. paper)
Subjects: LCSH: Coral reef animals--Juvenile literature. l Coral reef
  ecology--Juvenile literature. l Coral reefs and islands--Juvenile
  literature.
Classification: LCC QH95.8 (ebook) l LCC QH95.8 .K45 2018 (print) l DDC
  578.77/89--dc23
LC record available at https://lccn.loc.gov/2017022597

Editor: Marysa Storm/Megan Peterson
Designer: Patty Kelley
Photo Researcher/Producer: Shoreline Publishing Group LLC

Photo Credits:
Cover: Rafael Ben-Ari/Adobe Stock Images
Dreamstime.com: Seaphotoart 3; Hel080808 6; Alexey Stiop 12; Michael Elliott 16B; Mrtolc 16T; Anky10 16L. NOAA: 8. Shutterstock: John Walker 5; Chameleonseye 11; AndyPhotoStudio 15.

Printed in China.

HC 10 9 8 7 6 5 4 3 2 1
PB 10 9 8 7 6 5 4 3 2 1

What's under the water?

It's a coral reef.
Jane gets
her snorkel!
Let's explore!

The reef is near
the beach.
The water is warm.

Coral are alive.
They are
small animals.

Fish live in reefs.
Sara sees
some blue ones!

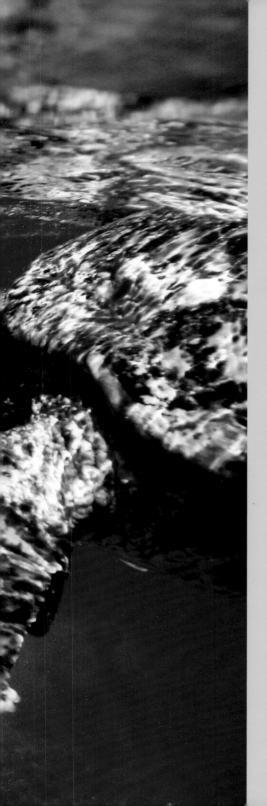

Other animals
live here, too.
Pat meets
a sea turtle!

Wow! That was a
great day.
Reefs are fun
to explore.

# CORAL REEF ANIMALS

sea star

sea horse

eel